Thoughts of Gold

Wisdom for Living from the Book of Proverbs

Brownlow Publishing Company, Inc.
6309 Airport Freeway, Fort Worth, Texas 76117

Thoughts of Gold

Wisdom for Living from the Book of Proverbs

LEROY BROWNLOW

BROWNLOW PUBLISHING COMPANY, INC.

FORT WORTH, TEXAS

Devotional & Gift Books

Flowers That Never Fade
Flowers of Friendship
Flowers for You
Flowers for Mother
A Father's World
Better Than Medicine — A Merry Heart
Making the Most of Life
Grandpa Was a Preacher
Thoughts of Gold — Wisdom for Living
With the Good Shepherd
Living With the Psalms — Devotions for Today
For Love's Sake
Today Is Mine
Leaves of Gold
In His Steps
The Fruit of the Spirit
Great Verses of the Bible
The Greatest Thing in the World
University of Hard Knocks
As A Man Thinketh
Children Won't Wait — A Parent's Prayer
In the Beginning — The Story of Creation
Give Us This Day — A Guide for Daily Living
For Mom With Love
Just Between Friends

Foreword

Solomon said, "A word fitly spoken is like apples of gold in pictures of silver" (Proverbs 25:11). But he was not discussing apples, gold, silver or pictures, but rather *words fitly spoken,* and words convey thoughts: so he was actually talking about *Thoughts of Gold* — thus the title of this book.

Thoughts of Gold: Wisdom for Living from the Book of Proverbs is a topical study of 86 major themes from Proverbs. Each theme is presented along with a practical, devotional essay followed by the relevant quotations from Proverbs.

The Proverbs of Solomon are wise, weighty and authoritative, many of which are common, household maxims the world over. His philosophical statements are recognized as the greatest collection of wisdom in all the world. There is nothing comparable to it. Thus it is wise that we as fallible wayfarers stick close to Solomon's guidelines as we map our course through a world that challenges the best within us.

Since all truth found in and among men originally came from God, then it behooves us to go to a book of wisdom written by the wisest man of all times — Solomon — as inspiration dictated. His basic principles of living are the ever-relevant and uncontroverted guidelines of success and happiness, for king or peasant, for young or old.

Believing that these thoughts deserve the term of *gold* and that they do provide *wisdom for living,* we offer them with the genuine desire that they will give direction and inspiration, hope and courage, success and security, to all who seek a richer and nobler life.

LEROY BROWNLOW

Do Rather Than Talk

Do!

Perform!

Don't just talk!

All talk and no accomplishment makes one a swaggering breath waster.

It's a shame the tongue doesn't tire as easily as the limbs and back. What a disgrace for there to be more *go* in the tongue than there is in the feet.

Man is like a watch: what he says doesn't amount to anything, if he never moves. A man's action tells us of his insides and of how wound up he is — tells us more than what he says.

Let us act, therefore, to bring our deeds in keeping with our words.

IN all labor there is profit: but the talk of the lips tendeth only to penury. — 14:23

THE sluggard is wiser in his own conceit than seven men that can render a reason. — 26:16

THE soul of the sluggard desireth, and hath nothing: but the soul of the diligent shall be made fat. — 13:4

9

Stand Up to Adversity

Adversity comes to everybody sooner or later. It slows all of us down for a while; it knocks many down, some get up, others stay down and get trampled. The person who get up the most times after being knocked down is the person who wins.

Taking heart to meet adversity can be our ladder whereby we climb to greater heights. Sorrow can turn to joy; poverty can lead to riches; and persecution can be the occasion for heroics. But we can't climb flat on our back. We'll have to get on our feet.

Many of our troubles are due to the world's dragging us; and they would end if we would stand up to them. Stand! Stand! And keep standing! And keep moving! It's hard to lose while on your feet.

IF thou faint in the day of adversity, thy strength is small. — 24:10

THE just shall come out of trouble. — 12:13

I have strength. — 8:14

Be Slow to Anger

Be calm. Hot heads boil fast and let off steam, wasting energy. We can't win in life's contest by squandering our energy in wild fury. Wrath is a victory for folly — defeat for the person.

Horace, the Latin poet who died in 8 B.C., said, "Anger is a short madness." A madness that prods one to say what he otherwise would not say. A madness that spurs one to do what he normally would not do. A madness that he later regrets.

One way to lessen our anger is to be in the right. People in the wrong get angry faster. Another way is to think. Some people use wrath as a substitute for thinking. And still a third way, be unselfish. The more self-centered one is, the more easily his temper is ignited.

> HE that is slow to anger is better than the mighty; and he that ruleth his spirit than he that taketh a city. — 16:32
>
> A wrathful man stirreth up strife: but he that is slow to anger appeaseth strife. — 15:18
>
> A stone is heavy, and the sand weighty; but a fool's wrath is heavier than them both. — 27:3
>
> AN angry man stirreth up strife, and a furious man aboundeth in transgression. — 29:22

11

Give Right Answers

If we open our mouth, we should do it wisely. If the answer is faulty, at least the tone can be soft. Of course, some questions don't deserve an answer.

Just as every mathematical sum has a right answer whether the mathematician knows it or not, so every human problem has a correct answer whether we give it or not. We may not always give it; for if we have all the answers, we haven't had all the questions. But we should try. And as we succeed, more questions will come — along with honor, success, and joy for us and the world.

> EVERY man shall kiss his lips that giveth a right answer. — 24:26

> THE lips of the wise shall preserve them. — 14:3

> THE heart of the righteous studieth to answer: but the mouth of the wicked poureth out evil things. — 15:28

> ANSWER not a fool according to his folly, lest thou also be like unto him. — 26:4

> SHE openeth her mouth with wisdom; and in her tongue is the law of kindness. — 31:26

Never Argue With Some People

A rash man said: "I know I'm ignorant. I'm glad I'm ignorant. I just hope I get ignoranter."

The resigning and gentle reply was, "I'm sure your ambition will be realized."

This was better than contending with him. Why reason with one we cannot help? Why argue with one who will later turn and rend us? It would be casting pearls before swine — allowing a fool to make a fool of us.

Some people can't argue. They can batter us with irony, cut us with sarcasm, smear us with acid, and blister us with anger, but they can't argue. They are good at appealing to prejudice, but poor at appealing to logic. And when they lose, they call us names.

IF a wise man contendeth with a foolish man, whether he rage or laugh, there is no rest. — 29:9

SPEAK not in the ears of a fool; for he will despise the wisdom of thy words. — 23:9

A fool hath no delight in understanding, but that his heart may discover itself. — 18:2

ANSWER not a fool according to his folly, lest thou also be like unto him. — 26:4

Don't Get Higher Than You Can Hold

To be picked up and placed high on the ladder of progress is no assurance that we won't get dizzy and fall off. However, ascending gradually gets us accustomed to the heights, and develops our muscles to hold.

Solid advancement is on the foundation we have laid. There set our ladder for the assurance the bottom won't drop out.

> Build today, then, strong and sure,
> With a firm and ample base;
> And ascending and secure
> Shall to-morrow find its place.
>
> — Henry Wadsworth Longfellow

Climbing has its perils (we may fall off), but staying on the ground has its hazards, too (something may fall on us). Climb, but don't climb faster than our strength will let us stay. And be nice to the people you pass on the way up, for you might need a friendly hand to break your fall on the way back down. With this spirit you are apt to stay.

> FOR better it is that it be said unto thee, come up hither; than that thou shouldest be put lower in the presence of the prince whom thine eyes have seen. — 25:7

Choose Good Associates

Every time we pick an associate we are picking a little piece of our own destiny. For there is power in associations. Evil associates corrupt good morals and destroy bright futures. Prodigality begins with naughty influence. Don't let the wrong people turn us into the wrong person. Don't permit corrupt associations to dissipate our youth, or debauch our middle age, or squander what could be our golden years.

It is smart to refuse a close association with those who would lead us into unfulfillment and forlorn hope. Life is too meaningful to allow the wasters of mankind to waste it.

THAT thou mayest walk in the ways of good men, and keep the paths of the righteous. — 2:20

BE not among winebibbers; among riotous eaters of flesh. — 23:20

GO from the presence of a foolish man, when thou perceivest not in him the lips of knowledge. — 14:7

MEDDLE not with them that are given to change. — 24:21

ENTER not into the path of the wicked, and go not in the way of evil men. Avoid it, pass not by it, turn from it, and pass away. — 4:14,15

15

Be Bold by Having Nothing to Hide

"Conscience does make cowards of us all," declared
Shakespeare. But when we haven't faulted or defaulted,
we can be bold. We won't flinch when associates speak
of an object that was stolen — we didn't take it. We
won't blush when friends speak of some ugly gossip
that was started — we had nothing to do with it. We
won't cringe when someone knocks on the door — we
haven't wronged anybody. We won't run when a
policeman stops in front of our house — we know he
is not after us.

This is more brave than seeking cover at the shuf-
fle of every leaf. Having nothing to hide, we have
nothing to fear. Unafraid, we can look every one in
the eye with confidence, peace, and joy.

Oh! how courage strengthens! And oh! how much
we need it!

> THE wicked flee when no man pursueth: but the
> righteous are bold as a lion. — 28:1
>
> BUT whoso hearkeneth unto me shall dwell safely, and
> shall be quiet from fear of evil. — 1:33
>
> THE way of the transgressor is hard. — 13:15

Avoid Bribes

Never take a bribe. Never give one. Let us not price ourselves down low enough to be bought, for we are worth too much. Likewise, do not price the other fellow up high enough to buy him, for he is not worth it.

A bribe has a repulsive stench which it acquired by being passed from one decay to another rot. Avoid it.

Right is not to be sold in the market. Favors are not to be auctioned to the highest bidder.

Remember — bribes and miseries go together. This is seen in the lowest and unhappiest man of all history — Judas. He took a bribe. He ended up a suicide.

A wicked man taketh a gift out of the bosom to pervert the ways of judgment. — 17:23

HE that is greedy of gain troubleth his own house; but he that hateth gifts shall live. — 15:27

THE king by judgment establisheth the land: but he that receiveth gifts overthroweth it. — 29:4

To have respect of persons is not good: for, for a piece of bread that man will transgress. — 28:21

Be Charitable

Charity begins at home, but it doesn't stay there. For charity is a virtue of the heart, not of geography. Charity is bighearted wherever it is — at home and away from home.

The benevolent heart, like the Good Samaritan, does more than talk. It acts. It hands over the needs. Professed love without charity is not love.

Remember — what we have will not do us any good unless it blesses us or somebody else.

And don't forget — we cannot help another without being helped. It is the law of returns.

SAY not unto thy neighbor, Go, and come again and to-morrow I will give; when thou hast it by thee. — 3:28

THE liberal soul shall be made fat: and he that watereth shall be watered also himself. — 11:25

HE that hath a bountiful eye shall be blessed; for he giveth of his bread to the poor. — 22:9

HE that giveth unto the poor shall not lack: but he that hideth his eyes shall have many a curse. — 28:27

SHE stretcheth out her hand to the poor; yea, she reacheth forth her hands to the needy. — 31:20

Never Dig Up Evil

Of course, we never dig up embarrassing sins on ourselves. It is always on the other fellow. And why uncover his shortcomings? Why dig to show up another when it is sure to become our own pit? If we drag a skeleton out of another's closet, it is sure to come alive and strike us. Just like a sleeping dog when roused will bite us.

If only those without sin are to do the digging, we can all put up our shovels.

It is smart to let buried evil rest! and rest! and rest! Never disturb it.

AN ungodly man diggeth up evil: and in his lips there is as a burning fire. — 16:27

A talebearer revealeth secrets: but he that is of a faithful spirit concealeth the matter. — 11:13

HE that passeth by, and meddleth with strife belonging not to him, is like one that taketh a dog by the ears. — 26:17

WHOSO diggeth a pit shall fall therein; and he that rolleth a stone, it will return upon him. — 26:27

Let Others Praise You

There are two things wrong with praising ourselves: It will not impress the people we wish to sway; and it is apt to be a solo.

The most laudable and effective way to acclaim self is to allow our works rather than our tongue to do it. A demonstration is real evidence while a tongue may be only sound — and that a repelling one from a strutting actor. When self-glory seeks glory, it never finds it. Instead, it finds mockery and repulsion as it stumbles around in its vanity and frustration.

LET another man praise thee, and not thine own mouth; a stranger, and not thine own lips. — 27:2

BE not wise in thine own eyes. — 3:7

SEEST thou a man wise in his own conceit? there is more hope of a fool than of him. — 26:12

IT is not good to eat much honey: so for men to search their own glory is not good. — 25:27

GIVE her of the fruit of her hands; and let her own works praise her in the gates. — 31:31

Profit From Correction

Nobody is perfect, so let's not pretend that we are. We gain nothing by being too proud to admit that we are wrong. If we are subject to error — and we are — we ought to be responsive to correction. If we can't be corrected, we can't get smarter, we can't get better, we can't advance — our condition is hopeless. But there is hope for the person who can be righted; he or she can admit error, and this is the starting point in all correction.

If we could all learn to accept correction and profit from it, we would need less of it!

CORRECTION is grievous unto him that forsaketh the way: and he that hateth reproof shall die. — 15:10

REPROOFS of instruction are the way of life. — 6:23

HE is in the way of life that keepeth instruction: but he that refuseth reproof erreth. — 10:17

WHOSO loveth instruction loveth knowledge: but he that hateth reproof is brutish. — 12:1

POVERTY and shame shall be to him that refuseth instruction: but he that regardeth reproof shall be honored. — 13:18

21

Seek Wise Counsel

One thing that distinguishes the wise and the foolish is their view of counsel. The wise person knows he doesn't know it all, while the fool thinks he does. Thinking he has all the answers and all the solutions, the fool thoughtlessly rushes into disaster; and another tragedy is that he never learns. He is fitter for mistakes than for counsel. He prefers to blunder on his own directions than to succeed on advice from others.

In contradistinction, the wise man is smart enough to get the best advice available before going into a project. Maybe this is why good luck blesses one and bad luck haunts the other.

> A wise man will hear, and will increase learning; and a man of understanding shall attain unto wise counsels. — 1:5
>
> WHERE no counsel is, the people fall: but in the multitude of counselors there is safety. — 11:14
>
> WITHOUT counsel purposes are disappointed: but in the multitude of counselors they are established. — 15:22
>
> HEAR counsel, and receive instruction, that thou mayest be wise in thy latter end. — 19:20
>
> EVERY purpose is established by counsel: and with good advice make war. — 20:18

Don't Fool Yourself by
Trying to Dupe Others

It was P. T. Barnum who said, "There's a sucker born every minute." Maybe so. And the biggest one of all is the person who thinks he can flimflam the public. Some he can, but some he can't; and even if he could fool all others, think what he's doing to self.

Abraham Lincoln philosophized: "You can fool some of the people all the time, and all of the people some of the time, but you cannot fool all of the people all of the time."

Man is smarter than a fish. Hiding the hook is no way to catch — at least, not to hold him.

Honesty needs no baiting.

STOLEN waters are sweet, and bread eaten in secret is pleasant. — 9:17

BREAD of deceit is sweet to a man; but afterward his mouth shall be filled with gravel. — 20:17

DECEIT is in the heart of them that imagine evil. — 12:20

THE folly of fools is deceit. — 14:8

BURNING lips and a wicked heart are like a potsherd covered with silver dross. — 26:23

Be Deliberate

Impulsiveness mortgages the future. Thinking liberates it, gives it to us unencumbered.

Weigh the facts. Make studied moves. Don't act rashly. Let's not leap before we think; if we do, we may have to be picked up in pieces. First ponder, then jump. Let wisdom's deliberation control the location and time of our jump. See if there is a soft landing.

We won't have to move so fast, if we get off shaky ground. Move over to something solid, and we can take more time to deliberate.

Furthermore, if we don't know whether we are coming or going, why be in such a hurry to get there?

PONDER the path of thy feet, and let all thy ways be established. — 4:26

THE thoughts of the diligent tend only to plenteousness; but of every one that is hasty only to want. — 21:5

SEEST thou a man that is hasty in his words? there is more hope of a fool than of him. — 29:20

24

Guard Against Despondency

Years ago a wife spent so much time counting what she didn't have that it eventually resulted in counting out her husband. He hasn't been heard from since. Her only joy was her despair.

A salesman, inclined to be despondent, built up a barrier of gloom between him and the buyers. Needless to say, he's no longer selling. Another victim of lost spirit.

Our mental attitude means much. The odds are we'll succeed, if we maintain a grateful, optimistic spirit. Let's be sure we count our blessings. I have never known a person to grow despondent while counting his blessings. It's his counting what he doesn't have that depresses him.

HEAVINESS in the heart of man maketh it stoop: but a good word maketh it glad. — 12:25

HOPE deferred maketh the heart sick: but when the desire cometh, it is a tree of life. — 13:12

A broken spirit drieth the bones. — 17:22

THE spirit of a man will sustain his infirmity; but a wounded spirit who can bear? — 18:14

25

Discuss Your Difference
With Your Neighbor

It is much better to talk over your breach with your neighbor than to go off and talk about him.

Dialogue may prove that we have no grievance at all, that things were not like they seemed. In that event, we regain a friend and spare ourselves from stewing in strife's boiling pot, fired in this instance by a false cause. If the face to face talk proves that our unhappy feelings are justified, it will present to the offender a ready opportunity to make amends.

Let the first move toward understanding and reconciliation be to our glory; and if we lose, we still win — a victory in principles.

DEBATE thy cause with thy neighbor himself; and discover not a secret to another. — 25:9

HE that is first in his own cause seemeth just; but his neighbor cometh and searcheth him. — 18:17

STRIVE not with a man without cause, if he have done thee no harm. — 3:30

BE not a witness against thy neighbor without cause. — 24:28

Be Discreet

Discretion is the knack to behave as common sense dictates. It is sensible, decent, circumspect, polite and politic. It manifests itself in words and deeds that seem virtuous, becoming and best. It is something the world demands. We can either fit in or be ruled out. And to foul out is such waste. Great ability without discretion is deplorable loss.

We have freedom of speech and freedom of conduct, and let's hope we have the judgment to know how to use them. Let us ponder our way. A short step of discretion is worth more than a long, fitful jump of inexpediency.

This is just another bit of wisdom Solomon gave the world:

> DISCRETION shall preserve thee, understanding shall keep thee. — 2:11
>
> KEEP sound wisdom and discretion. — 3:21
>
> THAT thou mayest regard discretion. — 5:2
>
> AS a jewel of gold in a swine's snout, so is a fair woman which is without discretion. — 11:22

Overlook the Mistreatment of Others

Each of us has too many faults to be grudgeful. Learn to pass over ill-treament, and we will have more peace and more friends.

We ought to be able to learn tolerance from intolerance, and forgiveness from vindictiveness. We don't want to be like the avengers. Oh! how hideous are the night riders of hate, bent on settling scores!

In passing over the transgressions of fellow creatures, we show a bigness bigger than little people who are out to get their enemies. To be wronged by another is small in comparison with wronging ourself by holding a grudge. Learning not just the words but the spirit of *Forgive us our debts as we forgive our debtors,* and a whole new world will open up to us.

THE discretion of a man deferreth his anger; and it is his glory to pass over a transgression. — 19:11

HE that covereth a transgression seeketh love; but he that repeateth (harpeth on) a matter separateth very friends. — 17:9

HATRED stirreth up strifes: but love covereth all sins — 10:12

28

Refuse to Be Mocked by Intoxicants

First the man takes a drink,
Then the drink takes a drink,
Then the drink takes the man.
— Japanese Proverb

Strong drink is a mocker. It has ridiculed millions as it stole away their brains and added to their troubles. With no regard for health or wealth, sanity or security, kinship or friendship, it has derided its victims by binding them to a restless bondage. Don't drink away your freedom.

And don't guzzle away your possibilities. Remember — the world has never seen the person who drank himself to health, prosperity, respect, and success.

No need to say more. Just look at a drunkard and you'll see more than any book can ever say.

WINE is a mocker, strong drink is raging: and whosoever is deceived thereby is not wise. — 20:1

FOR the drunkard and the glutton shall come to poverty. — 23:21

WHO hath woe? who hath sorrow? who hath contentions? who hath babbling? who hath wounds without cause? who hath redness of eyes? They that tarry long at the wine, they that go to seek mixed wine . . . At the last it biteth like a serpent, and stingeth like an adder. — 23:29-32

29

Watch Your Spending

Whatever you have, spend less.
— Samuel Johnson

What we spend is more important than what we make. Economy is the harder half of the battle of having, for it is harder to spend money wisely than to earn it. Use restraint. For there are more ways to spend money than there are to get it.

The instinct of self-preservation should urge us to curb our spending. There is no point in buying what we can't afford to impress people we don't like anyway. It is fatiguing to try to stay up with the other fellow — the chances are he is having a rough time trying to stay up with himself.

The love of economy is the root of all independence. When our ledger shows in black ink a little on the plus side, we can be more independent. Don't squander your freedom. It's foolish!

THERE is treasure to be desired and oil in the dwelling of the wise; but a foolish man spendeth it up. — 21:20

Be Kind to Your Enemies

How can we expect peace if we retaliate? How can we expect to live in a world of love if we keep a heart of hate? Of course, it is easier to fight back, take an eye for an eye, and a tooth for a tooth. But there are good reasons for overcoming this urge: One, to rise above the animal. Two, self-preservation, for if all enemies should slit each other's throat, there soon would be no one left.

Don't hold a grudge, for it will soon hold you.

The only satisfactory way to deal with our enemies is to be good to them. They don't know how to handle this tactic — those coals of fire we heap on their heads begin to burn — so they find it more comfortable to give in and become friends, that is if they are normal.

IF thine enemy be hungry, give him bread to eat; and if he be thirsty, give him water to drink: For thou shalt heap coals of fire upon his head, and the Lord shall reward thee. — 25:21,22

REJOICE not when thine enemy falleth, and let not thine heart be glad when he stumbleth. — 24:17

Fortify Against Enticement

George Washington said, "Few men have virtue enough to withstand the highest bidder." Let us belong to that strong few. *But how?*

Recognize temptation as a personal problem, one we have and one we must meet. No one can avoid being tempted, but we can stop yielding.

> Manlike it is to meet sin,
> Herolike it is to win.

Be farsighted. Look beyond wrong's temporary pleasure. See the reaping.

Avoid it. Don't expect it to go away while we keep beckoning it. Flee it.

Gain strength by overcoming, again and again. By resisting temptation we gain more strength to resist the next one.

My son, if sinners entice thee, consent thou not. — 1:10

For the lips of a strange woman drop as a honeycomb, and her mouth is smoother than oil: But her end is bitter as wormwood, sharp as a two-edged sword. — 5:3,4

The righteous is more excellent than his neighbor: but the way of the wicked seduceth them. — 12:26

A violent man enticeth his neighbor, and leadeth him into the way that is not good. — 16:29

Avoid Envy

A body of church officers voted to oust their long-time minister. When one was asked why he voted thus, he replied, "I don't know, except I'm tired of hearing his praises sung." Envy, born of self-love, cast that vote. Envy is spiteful. It's only satisfaction comes from hurting.

But envying what another has does not give us what we lack. It adds nothing. It is so futile. But more than futile, it is ugly and cruel, and those who are possessed by it will suffer for it. For envy has no happiness, no peace of mind, no bigness of soul, and no love, for "love envieth not." In Biblical thought, it makes us rotten on the inside. An ugly sight!

"Envy slays itself with its own arrows." It is a slow and horrible suicide. Let us not commit it.

A sound heart is the life of the flesh: but envy the rottenness of the bones. — 14:30

LET not thine heart envy sinners; but be thou i

EVIL

Foresee the Evil and Flee It

This injunction is a safety measure. When approaching the enemy, good soldiers are on the alert. Evil is out there. Always. In our own lives, the best way to overcome evil is to foresee it and flee it. Keeping away from the mire is wiser than wading through it.

Years ago a bedraggled drunkard decided to straighten up. And he did. But he continued to tie his horse to the hitching post outside the saloon. You guessed it. In time, he was back on the inside, drinking and reeling. He failed to foresee the danger of where he was tying his horse.

It is useless to pray, "Deliver us from evil," while we park our car just outside the door of it.

Let us pray for the insight to recognize evil, and the foresight to see it before we get there, and the will to turn back.

A prudent man foreseeth the evil, and hideth himself: but the simple pass on, and are punished. — 22:3

THORNS and snares are in the way of the froward: he that doth keep his soul shall be far from them. — 22:5

Give Reasons - Not Excuses

An excuse can be so ridiculous. For instance, a slothful man says, "A lion is in the streets." But nearly all excuses are so stupid that we wonder how they could come from intelligent people. It is easier for us to excuse than to accomplish, but not nearly as profitable. The excuse-maker makes excuses; the success-maker makes good.

Our moving world accepts no excuses. It runs off and leaves the alibier. The public won't buy it — might as well quit trying to sell it. We only accuse ourselves when we excuse ourselves.

And oftentimes excusing of a fault
Doth make the fault the worse by the excuse.
— William Shakespeare

Give a thousand reasons, but never an excuse.

THE slothful man saith, There is a lion without, I shall be slain in the streets. — 22:13

THE slothful man saith, There is a lion in the way; a lion is in the streets. — 26:13

Get the Facts

Getting the facts will save us from embarrassing blunders and unnecessary failures: bad business ventures, get-rich-quick schemes, unprofitable employment, ill-advised purchases, critical words, harsh judgments, coolness toward a friend, and many other grievous stupidities.

"Opinion is free, they tell us; but not if the opinion is false; for nothing is as costly as error. The good life cannot emerge from imperfect knowledge. We cannot go forward if our understanding is backward. We only begin to find fulfillment and prosperity as we deal in realities. Whatever future we have is in facts. If we build on the sands of misinformation, our structure is sure to fall.

> EVERY prudent man dealeth with knowledge: but a fool layeth open his folly. — 13:16
>
> THROUGH knowledge shall the just be delivered. — 11:9
>
> HE that hath knowledge spareth his words: and a man of understanding is of an excellent spirit. — 17:27
>
> THERE is a way which seemeth right unto a man; but the end thereof are the ways of death. — 14:12
>
> WITH all thy getting get understanding. — 4:7

See the Good

There are eyes that weep for the evil — blind to the good. Let us pray that they are not ours! Pray that our eyes do not drip with false lamentation while they silently pierce the heart of the offender.

One thing the human family has in common is imperfection — varying only in degrees. Thus it hardly befits any of us to be too critical. So may we never have the fault-finding, censorious, know-it-all, better-than-all, attitude. Going out with the magnifying glass in search of evil never rewards the searcher with appreciation or friends.

If we would look inside the person's shoe before we criticize the limp, we might not do it. Or if we would only see ourselves as others see us, we might see a beam so big in our eye that we would turn blind to our neighbor's mote.

In all candor, the critic needs to get some new eyes, some that are slanted toward good instead of evil, eyes that see from a righteous heart. That is the major problem.

> HE that hath a froward heart findeth no good: and he that hath a perverse tongue falleth into mischief. — 17:20

Avoid Flattery

Years ago I called on a man who was extremely lavish in praising me. When he stepped out of the room, I said to my associate, "I had better be wary of those compliments. I may not get out of here without their costing me."

Avoid flowery flatterers, for they are robbers in disguise. Beneath the appealing mask there is a manipulative exploiter ready to take advantage of an age-old weakness.

When we need advice, the worst kind comes from a flatterer who gives us unfounded hopes and inflated visions. We need the facts, and only a true person will give them to us.

WITH her much fair speech she caused him to yield, with the flattering of her lips she forced him. — 7:21

A flattering mouth worketh ruin. — 26:28

A man that flattereth his neighbor spreadeth a net for his feet. — 29:5

THEREFORE meddle not with him that flattereth with his lips. 20:19

Be Friendly

Robert Burns, the national poet of Scotland, went to church in a strange city where he received no word of welcome or friendly hand. Before leaving, he scrible these lines on the flyleaf of a hymnal:

> A cauld a wind as ever blew,
> A caulder kirk, and in't but few;
> As cauld a minister's e'er spak;
> Ye'll all be hot ere I come back!

The world is already too cold. We need to do our part to thaw it out. In a society of hostile forces and selfish unconcern, the warm, hearty disposition is most refreshing. The outstretched hand of friendliness is appreciated by man or beast.

All other things being equal, the friendly person will beat the unfriendly competitor in any profession. That magnetic, affable spirit always tips the balance in his favor.

Friendliness is truly one of the beauties of the world.

A man that hath friends must show himself friendly. — 18:24

PLEASANT words are as a honeycomb, sweet to the soul, and health to the bones. — 16:24

Make Friends Judiciously

How necessary and precious are honorable friend-
ships. We were not made to live alone. Our heart calls
for human ties. This puts a premium on good ones.

Choosing worthy friends, however, is not always
easy. But succeed in this, and we are apt to miss the
follies and the shame that comes from being in league
with cheap persons. Pick a friend so pure that it will
be hard for you to be false.

The Book of Proverbs instructs us:

MAKE no friendship with an angry man; and with a
furious man thou shalt not go; lest thou learn his ways,
and get a snare to thy soul. — 22:24,25

HE that walketh with wise men shall be wise: but a com-
panion of fools shall be destroyed. — 13:20

BE not thou envious against evil men, neither desire to
be with them. — 24:1

HE that loveth pureness of heart, for the grace of his lips
the king shall be his friend. — 22:11

OINTMENT and perfume rejoice the heart: so doth the
sweetness of a man's friend by hearty counsel. — 27:9

Give Gifts

The open hand is more effective than the clinched fist. It is easier to run life's gauntlet, if we drop a few gifts along the way. While they are being picked up, there can be no hostilities.

Gifts open hearts, doors and purses. I learned this when I was a little boy. A man would come to the door and say, "Mrs. Brownlow, I have something I would like to show you." She would reply, "No, thank you, I'm not interested." Another would come and say, "Lady, I have a little gift for you." My mother would open the door and invite him in. Before he left, he sold her something.

Little gifts, given out of genuine appreciation, make lots of room for us — room in crowded spaces and in busy schedules.

EVERY man is a friend to him that giveth gifts. — 19:6

A man's gift maketh room for him, and bringeth him before great men. — 18:16

A gift is a precious stone in the eyes of him that hath it: whithersoever it turneth, it prospereth. — 17:8

A gift in secret pacifieth anger: and a reward in the bosom, strong wrath. — 21:14

Refuse to Listen to Gossip

There is a time when we all think no one should listen to gossip — when it is about us. Fairness and brotherly love require each to give the same consideration to the other fellow who is maligned.

I have counselled thousands in personal matters, and experience has taught me that nearly all rumors are different from the facts. If it is wrong to have a gossipy tongue, then it is also wrong to have gossipy ears. One would cease without the other.

Wouldn't the following be more inspiring?

> *Wouldn't this old world be better*
> *If the folk we met would say,*
> *"I have something good to tell you!"*
> *And with joy tell it that way?*
>
> *Wouldn't it be sweet and helpful,*
> *If each greeting, warm and true,*
> *Carried with it this assurance,*
> *"I have something good to tell you!"*

But rumor-mongering tongues keep wagging, and slimy ears keep reaching out to hear. Why? There is an affinity there — wickedness.

> A wicked doer giveth heed to false lips; and a liar giveth ear to a naughty tongue. — 17:4

Don't Be a Gossiper

The gossiper smears names, drives wedges, and destroys harmonious relations — ever harms, never helps. Gossip is an easy villainy. It is easy to run a person down. Hesiod who lived about 700 B.C. said:

> Gossip is mischievous, light and easy to raise,
> but grievous to bear and hard to get rid of.

The tattler is known as a busybody, a meddler in the affairs of others. The whisperer is never appreciated, for if he tattles to you, he will tattle about you.

Gossip indicates immaturity or malice. It is done either without thinking (immaturity) or with calculated thinking to hurt another (malice). If we do it, we force others to conclude we are immature or full of hate.

Tattling doesn't require brains — just a loose tongue, a constant stream of ill words from an inexhaustible spring with little wisdom in it. We should have more sense than the family parrot.

He that covereth a transgression seeketh love; but he that repeateth a matter separateth very friends. — 17:9

A froward man soweth strife: and a whisperer separateth chief friends. — 16:28

THE words of a talebearer are as wounds. — 18:8

43

Avoid Being Greedy

Little Johnny ate all the cake. When asked why he didn't think of his little sister, he replied, "I did think of her. I thought she might come before I got through." This is greed's way.

We all remember the story of the greedy man who tried to swim a river with a bag of gold. Rather than turn loose, he drowned. Again, this is greed's way — to drown in a sea of self.

If we allow greed to control us, we will turn a demon loose in our own soul. We blow out the ray of hope for a beautiful life, and permit our ugliness to stumble in darkness. Avarice is so loathsome that he who lives only to get blesses the world when he leaves.

> HE that is greedy of gain troubleth his own house. — 15:27

> HE that oppresseth the poor to increase his riches, and he that giveth to the rich, shall surely come to want. — 22:16.

> HE that maketh haste to be rich shall not be innocent. — 28:20

> HE that hasteth to be rich hath an evil eye, and considereth not that poverty shall come upon him. — 28:22

> BETTER is a little with righteousness, than great revenues without right. — 16:8

Refuse to Believe Everything

If you fool me when I don't think, shame on you for your deceit, and shame on me for my gullibility. Only little children and naive adults believe everything they are told.

A little boy is told that he can catch a bird by sprinkling salt on its feathers, and he starts out with a handful of salt. Sometimes his parents are told something just as fantastic, and they, too, swallow it.

One day during World War II, I was in downtown Fort Worth and a paper boy barked in the customary tone, "Submarine comes up Trinity River and shells Fort Worth." (That wasn't in the paper.) A lady turned pale, grabbed her heart, gasped, and muttered, "Oh, my." She never thought of the impossibility of the boy's attention-rouser. The way the river runs, it is perhaps seven hundred miles to the gulf, marked with sharp bends, shallow places, and narrow widths. Unthinking, undiscerning, she accepted what she heard.

Weigh what you are told. Is it reasonable? Rational? Hear every man; but while you listen, keep clear the windows of the mind and see beyond the words.

THE simple believeth every word: but the prudent man looketh well to his going. — 14:15

45

Don't Harm Yourself by
Harming Others

What a lesson! If our society could just learn that there is no way for us to willfully harm another without hurting ourselves. If we dig a pit to entrap another, we are apt to fall in it; and if we roll a stone to crush another, there is a good chance it will roll back on us. The law of consequence has no exceptions. Hurt others and we will suffer. The way of the harmer is hard.

It is more noble, neighborly, and self-serving to be big and helpful.

WHOSO diggeth a pit shall fall therein: and he that rolleth a stone, it will return upon him. — 26:27

WHOSO causeth the righteous to go astray in an evil way, he shall fall himself into his own pit: but the upright shall have good things in possession. — 28:10

FROWARDNESS is in his heart, he deviseth mischief continually; he soweth discord. Therefore shall his calamity come suddenly; suddenly shall he be broken without remedy. — 6:14,15

THE righteousness of the upright shall deliver them: but transgressors shall be taken in their own naughtiness. — 11:6

Wait for the Light to Turn Green

Whoever dashes yon and hither
May watch his cherished plans all wither
And find that any kind of dither
Is waste.

— Marjorie Lindsey Brewer

"Make haste slowly," is the good practical advice given a long time ago by Augustus Caesar.

It is unwise to:
— Grab the bait before we consider the hook.
— Make strife without counting the cost.
— Censure before we get the facts.
— Speak before we think.
— Plant before the ground is ready.
— Move into the intersection when the light is red.

Don't be too hasty. Think it through. Then act.

HE that is hasty of spirit exalteth folly. — 14:29

HE that hasteth with his feet sinneth. — 19:2

SEEST thou a man that is hasty in his words? there is more hope of a fool than of him. — 29:20

GO not forth hastily to strive, lest thou know not what to do in the end thereof, when thy neighbor hath put thee to shame. — 25:8

47

Keep Your Heart Pure

It is the heart that matters most. When Sir Walter Raleigh was being led to the block to be beheaded, the executioner asked him which way he would like for his head to lie. He replied, "It matters little how the head lies, provided the heart is right."

On my grandmother's farm there was a spring. What flowed from it was what was in it. So it is with the stream of life: the behavior that flows is from the heart. Out of it are the issues of life.

We are no stronger or better than our heart; as is our heart, so are we. Keep our hearts pure, our lives cannot be otherwise.

Keep thy heart with all diligence; for out of it are the issues of life. — 4:23

A sound heart is the life of the flesh. — 14:30

For as he thinketh in his heart, so is he. — 23:7

Hear thou, my son, and be wise, and guide thine heart in the way. — 23:19

Be Honest

It pays to be honest, but some people don't think it pays enough. I knew a filling station owner who changed his pumps to give short measure. But it didn't pay. He went broke. He who resorts to short change, less weight, misrepresentation, or any other unscrupulousness, is sure to fail. Interchange requires confidence, which cannot exist long where dishonesty prevails.

Honesty is the foundation of character, and without it life is sure to cave in. Honesty is the basis of every worthwhile success. It is success! What an honor to be an "honest man"! Not for the sake of policy, but for the sake of right!

A false balance is abomination to the Lord: but a just weight is his delight. — 11:1

DIVERS weights are an abomination unto the Lord; and a false balance is not good. — 20:23

REMOVE not the ancient landmark, which thy fathers have set. — 22:28

THE integrity of the upright shall guide them: but the perverseness of transgressors shall destroy them. — 11:3

Avoid the Bread of Idleness

There is nothing in the world as demoralizing as idleness.

Sluggards say they are tired, and maybe they are, but it is never true of their stomachs. They fold their hands, but not their wants. They sleep, but their needs never slumber.

All of us have needs. Our distinction is in filling them. Other things equal, plenty or poverty is as simple as this: Fold your hands and want, or busy your hands and have. It is left up to us, the keepers of the earth.

> YET a little sleep, a little slumber, a little folding of the hands to sleep: So shall thy poverty come as one that traveleth, and thy want as an armed man. — 6:10,11
>
> THE way of the slothful man is a hedge of thorns. — 15:19
>
> LOVE not sleep, lest thou come to poverty: open thine eyes, and thou shalt be satisfied with bread. — 20:13
>
> SHE riseth also while it is yet night, and giveth meat to her household, and a portion to her maidens. — 31:15
>
> SHE looketh well to the ways of her household, and eateth not the bread of idleness. — 31:27

Take Instruction

"You can't tell him anything," is a sad comment often heard. A rejection of help! How tragic!

Instruction is better than gold. We spend the gold, but instruction will help us make some more. Keep instruction and it will keep you, provided it is accurate. If it's not, our problems will be compounded. It's easy to get advice, but the people who are so free with it are more in need of it than we are.

Get advice! Get good advice! And take it! Remember the words of the wise old Benjamin Franklin: "They that will not be counselled cannot be helped."

TAKE fast hold of instruction; let her not go: keep her; for she is thy life. — 4:13

RECEIVE my instruction, and not silver; and knowledge rather than choice gold. — 8:10

POVERTY and shame shall be to him that refuseth instruction: but he that regardeth reproof shall be honored. — 13:18

UNDERSTANDING is a wellspring of life unto him that hath it: but the instruction of fools is folly. — 16:22

GIVE instruction to a wise man, and he will be yet wiser. — 9:9

Stay Free of Jealousy

Jealousy is madness that knows no bounds.
It is unreasonableness that knows no limits.
It is suspicion that always suspects.
It is misery that is forever miserable.
It is ever busy, but never does the right thing. In its ungoverned hurry to keep, it drives away.
It can be a monster without cause, feeding on nothing but itself.

> *But jealous souls will not be answer'd so;*
> *They are not ever jealous for the cause,*
> *But jealous for they are jealous; 'tis a monster*
> *Begot upon itself, born on itself.*
>
> — William Shakespeare

It is a deadly venom, which poisons and kills beautiful relationships.

> *The venom clamors of a jealous woman*
> *Poison more deadly than a mad dog's tooth.*
>
> — William Shakespeare

Simply put, it has a special knack for making a fool of itself.

> For jealousy is the rage of man: therefore he will not spare in the day of vengeance. — 6:34

Use Good Judgment

Abraham Lincoln said, "When you have got an elephant by the hind leg, and he is trying to run away, it's best to let him run." In other words, use a little judgment. The reason some people get trampled and dragged through life is they don't know when to turn loose. And the reason some others never get anywhere is they don't know when to take hold.

Judgment, call it what you will, is but common sense. And how frightening for one to be learned without it. With more education and less judgment, he is prepared to excel in only plain, undraped madness.

Use judgment. Take a feather and throw it in the air and see which way the wind is blowing.

Think. Pray. Sleep on a matter and then make the decision.

> Much food is in the tillage of the poor: but there is that is destroyed for want of judgment. — 13:23
>
> Wisdom is too high for a fool. — 24:7
>
> Keep sound wisdom and discretion: So shall they be life unto thy soul, and grace to thy neck. Then shalt thou walk in thy way safely, and thy foot shall not stumble. — 3:21-23

Be Just in All Our Dealings

In the long run, the fair and evenhanded have always come out ahead of the unjust. There are no shortcuts. The unjust think so, but eventually they find injustice a long rocky road cursed with disappointment and failure.

All people occasionally get knocked down, but those known for fair play can rise again.

The initial price of justice is sometimes very high, but it is always a bargain; for what you can't do without is never too expensive. Pay it. Society won't let you get by without it.

BUT the path of the just is as the shining light, that shineth more and more unto the perfect day. — 4:18

BLESSINGS are upon the head of the just. — 10:6

HE that walketh uprightly walketh surely: but he that perverteth his ways shall be known. — 10:9

THE wicked is snared by the transgression of his lips: but the just shall come out of trouble. — 12:13

FOR a just man falleth seven times, and riseth up again: but the wicked shall fall into mischief. — 24:16

Don't Justify the Wicked or Condemn the Just

Justice is no respecter of persons.
— John Wise

Justice is the great interest of a man on earth.
— Daniel Webster

He who justifies the wicked and condemns the just outrages justice. It tears apart the ligament that holds civilization together. There is nothing right about it.

But some people are on the wrong side of nearly everything. They praise the wicked. They smear the just. But their calling sweet bitter, and bitter sweet, changes nothing. All they do is debase themselves further. But regardless of how vocal evil is in its self-laudation, it still condemns itself by the lives of its children; and by the same rule of exemplification, righteousness is praised by hers.

Putting on the wrong label is sheer nonsense. Truth doesn't change. And facts are still facts.

HE that justifieth the wicked, and he that condemneth the just, even they both are abomination to the Lord. — 17:15

THEY that forsake the law praise the wicked: but such as keep the law contend with them. — 28:4

Learn From Little Things of Nature

Many of the little things of nature are exceedingly wise, wise enough to survive the hostile forces about them; and if we are smart, we shall learn from them some of the world's most needed lessons:

We shall learn to prepare in summer for the winter. We won't wait until the snow falls to get ready for it.

We shall be instructed to build on a good foundation. While the sand invites play, we shall learn better than to build upon it.

We shall master the need of cooperation. Little forces combined create an overwhelming power.

We shall ascertain the necessity of work. It is the means of attainment.

THERE be four things which are little upon the earth, but they are exceeding wise:

THE ants are a people not strong, yet they prepare their meat in the summer;

THE conies are but a feeble folk, yet make they their houses in the rocks;

THE locusts have no king, yet go they forth all of them by bands;

THE spider taketh hold with her hands, and is in kings' palaces. — 30:24-28

Be on the Right End of Loans

"Easy payments"? For which one? the borrower or the lender?

The human species, according to the best theory I can form of it, is composed of two distinct races, the men who borrow, and the men who lend.

— Charles Lamb

It is better to be the lender than the borrower. The borrower has a double debt to pay, the principal and the interest. The lender receives the interest, which gives him a servant who provides him income while he sleeps. If you are in debt, someone owns a part of you. Debt and servitude have the same address. So the less one borrows, the less time he has to spend on servitude's row.

It takes much discipline to save money, to be on the lending end of loans, to refuse to join the procession of spendthrifts rushing to obligate themselves for things they don't need. But a refusal will give you more in the long run. Try it. Even your sleep will improve.

THE rich ruleth over the poor, and the borrower is servant to the lender. — 22:7

Think Before You Speak

Much of life calls for deliberation.

Don't wag a rash tongue. Noise is not enough.

Think! As Thomas Jefferson said, "For God's sake let us freely hear both sides." When we consider there may be other viewpoints or sensitive feelings held by another, it should refrain the tongue until thought takes hold.

Think! Don't let our tongue go faster than our brain. If we think twice before we speak, our speech will be twice as good — and maybe more than twice as brief.

A fool uttereth all his mind: but a wise man keepeth it in till afterward. — 29:11

SEEST thou a man that is hasty in his words? there is more hope of a fool than of him. — 29:20

THE heart of the wise teacheth his mouth, and addeth learning to his lips. — 16:23

HE that answereth a matter before he heareth it, it is folly and shame unto him. — 18:13

WHOSO keepeth his mouth and his tongue, keepeth his soul from troubles. — 21:23

Build a Circle of Love

The more we love the closer we approach the likeness of God.

Build a circle of love. For love changes things. It converts a shack into a palace, and turns a hamburger into a feast. It smooths the rocky road, and pulls down the hills. It gives courage because it stands with us. It makes pain less painful, sorrow less sorrowful, and joy more joyful. It takes some of the disappointment out of failure, and puts more delight in success. It does because of its ability to share, and much of what life is all about is sharing.

A ray of love is what we all need — to give it and to receive it. So, let love shine and shine and shine, in me and on you, in you and on me.

I love them that love me. —, 8:17

LOVE covereth all sins. — 10:12

BETTER is a dinner of herbs where love is, than a stalled ox and hatred therewith. — 15:17

A friend loveth at all times, and a brother is born for adversity. — 17:17

Be Mannerly Around Another's Table

Don't be a glutton, especially if the other fellow is paying for it. We would resent being called a pig; but if we are piggish, then the designation, though unkind, is descriptive.

Good manners make us more welcome.

Manners express a relation status; and if we want the relation to be appreciated, then enhance it with good breeding. Good manners is the self-control to say, "No, thank you," when we still have an appetite, especially if the platter is getting empty.

Bad manners show we are fonder of the food than of those present. This puts an unnecessary strain on their manners, as Wendell Wilkie said: "The test of good manners is to be able to put up pleasantly with bad ones." It is savage to subject our host to this test.

To eat is animal; to eat with restraint is human — maybe a little divine.

WHEN thou sittest to eat with a ruler, consider diligently what is before thee. And put a knife to thy throat, if thou be a man given to appetite. — 23:1,2

Be Merciful

Teach me to feel another's woe,
To hide the fault I see;
That mercy I to others show,
That mercy show to me.

Justice without mercy is cold-blooded. Justice follows the letter of the law, mercy lets you read between the lines. And there are more extenuating circumstances between the lines than cruel, vengeful people can see. Cold bloody eyes can see only the decree's cold, black type.

Have a heart. Season justice with compassion. We are not apt to get what we don't give. Sooner or later we will be needing a little leniency. And if we get justice we might be hanged; but a touch of humanity will give us another chance.

HE that followeth after righteousness and mercy findeth life, righteousness, and honor. — 21:21

HE that oppresseth the poor reproacheth his Maker: but he that honoreth him hath mercy on the poor. — 14:31

LET not mercy and truth forsake thee: bind them about thy neck; write them upon the table of thine heart. — 3:3

THE merciful man doeth good to his own soul; but he that is cruel troubleth his own flesh. — 11:17

Keep a Merry Disposition

Cheerfulness is one of the most profitable of all traits. It makes life more livable to the person who has it, not to mention how much better it makes life for those around him.

We don't have to wait for the joyous spirit to reward us. It pays now: promotes health, sparks vigor in the mind, and converts homeliness into a winning grace. It fills the heart with harmony, produces thankfulness, and strengthens our life for every twist of fate.

We can climb higher and last longer with an easy and cheerful frame of mind.

Truly it will give us a big advantage over the person who doesn't have it.

> HE that is of a merry heart hath a continual feast. — 15:15
>
> A merry heart maketh a cheerful countenance: but by sorrow of the heart the spirit is broken — 15:13
>
> A merry heart doeth good like a medicine: but a broken spirit drieth the bones. — 17:22
>
> HEAVINESS in the heart of man maketh it stoop. — 12:25
>
> MAKE my heart glad. — 27:11

62

Don't Be a Contentious Drip

Continual nagging is not justifiable.

Even though we don't accept a thing, we don't have to be an annoying drip. After a while shut up. We won't gain anything by nagging. There is no need to go on and on; if we do, one thing is sure to stop — love and friendship. Don't be so foolhardy as to repel the very thing you want. While nagging brings an ugly joy to some people, it is not worth the price they have to pay for it.

Maybe we are right. Maybe the one we nag is wrong. But we are undoubtedly wrong in pestering a person. Let up. You can't be a drip without splattering somebody, and he won't like it. He just might remove himself from the splash. Try another approach. Silence has its victories, too.

THE contentions of a wife are a continual dropping. — 19:13

A continual dropping in a very rainy day and a contentious woman are alike. — 27:15

IT is better to dwell in the wilderness, than with a contentious and an angry woman. — 21:19

Be a Good Neighbor

There are things to do and not do:

— Speak cheerfully to him.

— Treat him with appreciation.

— Be short on advice.

— When needed, lend him a helping hand.

— "Love him," as Benjamin Franklin suggested, "but don't pull down your hedge."

— Don't weary him.

— Don't regard him as a cup to be drained.

— Don't be nosy.

— Don't speak all we know or judge all we see.

FOR better is a neighbor that is near than a brother far off. — 27:10

DEVISE not evil against thy neighbor, seeing he dwelleth securely by thee. — 3:29

HE that is void of wisdom despiseth his neighbor: but a man of understanding holdeth his peace. — 11:12

WITHDRAW thy foot from thy neighbor's house; lest he be weary of thee, and so hate thee. — 25:17

Try Not to Offend

No one can mix and mingle and carry on the ordinary affairs of life without occasionally giving offense. We are too imperfect never to blunder. But do not use your frailty to justify your unrestraint as you thoughtlessly trample the feelings of others.

The Golden rule, *Do unto others as you would have them do unto you,* requires us not to willfully hurt any one's feelings.

The Second Commandment, *Love your neighbor as you love yourself,* demands that we be considerate of their sensitivity.

It is easy to be thoughtless and clumsy. So let us consider some additional precautions:

— Don't show him up. This deflates.
— Don't ridicule him. This hurts his pride.
— Don't bully him. He wants to act on his own.
— Don't exploit him. He is not merchandise.

Positively, manifest good will, courtesy, and a little forethought. This is easier than winning back the offended.

A brother offended is harder to be won than a strong city: and their contentions are like the bars of a castle. — 18:19

Let Not Pleasure Impoverish You

That man is richest whose pleasures are cheapest.

— Henry David Thoreau

Every man is his own architect and builds his own house of pleasure. If it stands, it must consist of more than idleness, extravagance, lust and dissipation.

What some call pleasure is very fleeting and unsatisfying, aptly expressed by Robert Burns:

> *But pleasures are like poppies spread —*
> *You seize the flow'r, its bloom is shed;*
> *Or like the snow falls in the river —*
> *A moment white — then melts forever.*

If we want real pleasure, hold down the trouble, the cost, the time and the intemperance; that which takes too much of any of these is disappointing.

We don't have to look for the most satisfying pleasures. They are everywhere. All we have to do is to tune our heart to enjoy them — friends and relatives, books and art, work and rest, summer and winter, fields and woods, rivers and lakes, mountains and seas, flowers and trees, are but a few of them. Enjoy them rationally.

> HE that loveth pleasure shall be a poor man: he that loveth wine and oil shall not be rich. — 21:17

Keep on Praying Terms With God

How lovely are the lips of those who talk acceptably to God.

If we do, that is a major accomplishment within itself. Not everybody is harmonious enough with God to get an audience with Him. It would be unbecoming for one to say, "Lord, Lord," when his heart is far from Him; or to say, "Lord, Lord," and do not what He says.

God is not a jumping bellboy or tip-seeking redcap, ready to move at the least beckoning gesture. His ears are open only to the righteous and obedient who call upon him sincerely and reverently.

Our need for divine help may become awfully acute. Better keep the line open to *Him*. We may need to make more than just a local call.

THEN shall they call upon me, but I will not answer; they shall seek me early, but they shall not find me: For that they hated knowledge, and did not choose the fear of the Lord: They would none of my counsel: they despised all my reproof. — 1:28-30

THE Lord is far from the wicked: but he heareth the prayer of the righteous. — 15:29

67

Live Like You Pray

It insults God to live one way and pray another. He who seeks the blessings of God should also seek the will of God. As we pray, "Give us this day our daily bread," it is incumbent upon us to live the spirit of, "Thy will be done on earth as it is in heaven."

It is vain for a farmer to pray, "God drop my bread out of heaven, ready to eat, now." This disrespects the law God has established for obtaining food. It is an abomination. It is equivalent to asking God to set aside His will to obey our will. He won't do it.

Alfred Tennyson said, "More things are wrought by prayer than this world dreams of." Right. But think how many things are wrought by living and doing. The hands that help are doing the will of God the same as the lips that pray. Frankly, effective praying requires a little more than bending knees and moving lips: like turning a hand, and changing the heart. We need to pray with our works as well as our words.

Getting through to God depends more on obedient ears than on an expressive tongue.

> HE that turneth away his ear from hearing the law, even his prayer shall be abomination. — 28:9

Rise Above Prejudice

Use our brains — not our prejudices! Most of us are so prejudiced that we hate to acknowledge any one has good sense who does not not agree with us.

One of the drags on progress through the centuries is prejudice. Without an open mind man has a closed future. A closed mind is like a closed door that has to be opened from within by its possessor. And he will never do it until he decides that his thinking a thing is right does not make it right, and that there are other views beside the biased ones formed by his limited experiences.

Let's not just rearrange our prejudices. Brush those chips off our shoulders. Then we can walk straighter. Don't go through life bent over beneath a burden of prejudgments. For the sake of fairness hear the other side.

ALL the ways of a man are clean in his own eyes. — 16:2

EVERY way of a man is right in his own eyes. — 21:2

THERE is a way which seemeth right unto a man; but the end thereof are the ways of death. — 14:12

THE way of a fool is right in his own eyes: but he that hearkeneth unto counsel is wise. — 12:15

Resist Pride

Pride is an ever-defeating vice. It eats up a person, leaving very little to admire. The proud are disliked — especially by the proud. In contrast, the world loves the humble — not the humble that are proud of it, but the really humble.

Pride is the vain and exalted disposition that produces strife, hypocrisy, ostentation, and a restlessness that is never satisfied.

The nose-in-the-air look causes some to overlook many of the opportunities of life which originate in the lower beginnings. Appearing to be too big for some of the humble callings will not make us bigger, but will rather shrink our size, and our fortune, and our peace.

PRIDE goeth before destruction, and a haughty spirit before a fall. — 16:18

WHEN pride cometh, then cometh shame: but with the lowly is wisdom. — 11:2

BETTER it is to be of an humble spirit with the lowly, than to divide the spoil with the proud. — 16:19

ONLY by pride cometh contention: but with the well advised is wisdom. — 13:10

A man's pride shall bring him low: but honor shall uphold the humble in spirit. — 29:23

Push Straight Ahead

If we would succeed, finish a task and be done with it.

I know a man who has never accomplished much. The reason is he quits before he completes a job — many jobs but few accomplishments. If all his efforts were put in straight course pursuits, this unfortunate man would be a champion achiever.

A good bird dog sticks with hunting birds; he doesn't take off after a rabbit. What a shame when a dog is more disciplined and unified in purpose than a man.

Let us ponder and establish our goals. Then pursue them with singleness, turning neither to the left nor the right. Don't listen to the whispers of fancy. Don't give ear to the side calls. Pass up the phantoms — leave them to the quickies who have an eye for the unreal. Be not diverted!

> LET thine eyes look right on, and let thine eyelids look straight before thee. Ponder the path of thy feet, and let all thy ways be established. Turn not to the right hand nor to the left . . . — 4:25-27

> As a bird that wandereth from her nest, so is a man that wandereth from his place. — 27:8

71

Plan to Reap What You Sow

Today we sow. Tomorrow we reap. Plan on it. For the universal law of sowing and reaping is unalterable.

> *The tissue of the life to be,*
> *We weave with colors all our own;*
> *And on the fields of destiny*
> *We reap as we have sown.*

The thought of reaping what we sow may persuade us to change our sowing. Sow wild oats, and we reap a crop that has already flooded the market. Sow the wind, and we reap a whirlwind. But sow the good life, and pleasant days we shall have.

Many a person has wished at harvest time that he had sown a different crop, but it was too late. Sow now what you want later.

THE wicked worketh a deceitful work: but to him that soweth righteousness shall be a sure reward. — 11:18

HE that troubleth his own house shall inherit the wind. — 11:29

HE that soweth iniquity shall reap vanity: and the rod of his anger shall fail. — 22:8

Don't Expect Something for Nothing

We can't have something without its costing somebody something.

Nature has its laws of recompense, granting plenty to the laborer and poverty to the idler. Nature says, "If you would have the fruit, care for the tree; or if you would have bread, till the soil; or if you prefer unnecessary sleep, learn to do it on an empty stomach." It tells us that the worker is worthy of his hire and that the idler is deserving of his want.

Creation's universal law of cause and consequence is unalterable. He that sows sparingly shall reap also sparingly. It is foolish to try to change it or ignore it; so if we are unwilling to work, we should not expect to eat.

WHOSO keepeth the fig tree shall eat the fruit thereof; so he that waiteth on his master shall be honored. — 27:18

HE that tilleth his land shall have plenty of bread: but he that followeth after vain persons shall have poverty enough. — 28:19

THE recompense of a man's hands shall be rendered unto him. — 12:14

THE soul of the sluggard desireth, and hath nothing; but the soul of the diligent shall be made fat. — 13:4

Think of Your Reputation

Better check up on the man who doesn't care about his reputation. Indeed, what people think of you doesn't alter you, but it can help or hurt you. Thus the man concerned with his reputation is interested in himself. That man is my choice.

During the Great Depression a local boy of eighteen was given a teaching job in the public school in preference to forty-nine other applicants. He had lettered in athletics, represented the school in speech contests, maintained high grades, and had been selected all-around student three years. Furthermore, when the church needed a speaker he was available. His reputation got the job.

The third surest support is reputation. First, God. Second, character. Third, what people think of you — this often makes the difference.

A good name is rather to be chosen than great riches, and loving favor rather than silver and gold. — 22:1

HER husband is known in the gates, when he sitteth among the elders of the land. — 31:23

EVEN a child is known by his doings, whether his work be pure, and whether it be right. — 20:11

THE memory of the just is blessed: but the name of the wicked shall rot. — 10:7

Have a Stronger God Than Riches

Riches are like the birds: they have wings, and no one knows when flying time will come. It is better to have a god that won't fly away.

Riches are a strong servant, but a weak god. To keep the riches serving you:

— Don't be too trustful in holding.
— Don't be too anxious in keeping.
— Don't be too greedy in multiplying.
— Don't be too sorrowful in losing.

All rich people can testify that riches are not as satisfying as the poor people think. They are like the little hard-shell pecans we gathered when I was a boy. We tore our clothes in getting them, stained our hands in handling them, broke our teeth in cracking them, but never filled our stomachs with eating them.

WILT thou set thine eyes upon that which is not? for riches certainly make themselves wings; they fly away as an eagle toward heaven. — 23:5

RICHES profit not in the day of wrath. — 11:4

HE that trusteth in his riches shall fall. — 11:28

FOR riches are not for ever. — 27:24

THE eyes of man are never satisfied. — 27:20

Put Right Ahead of Riches

Whether it means riches or rags, always do right.

Horace wrote many centuries ago, "Make money, money by fair means if you can, if not, by any means money." Unfortunately, this has too long been the corrupting principle of too many people.

I am for wealth, but not at any price. It makes no sense for the purse to get fatter while the heart gets leaner. It is better to be right than rich. The wealthiest wealth is in living, and he who lives best is the richest. Let us look at our hearts along with our ledger.

What an honor for it to be said of a person, in the language of Dryden, "Large was his wealth, but larger was his heart."

BETTER is a little with righteousness, than great revenues without right. — 16:8

BETTER is the poor that walketh in his uprightness, than he that is perverse in his ways, though he be rich. — 28:6

HE that hasteth to be rich hath an evil eye, and considereth not that poverty shall come upon him. — 28:22

Place Goodness Before Sacrifice

Goodness is more excellent than sacrifice.

Rich gifts turn poor when they are pretentious acts of self-seeking men. How right we are is more important than how much we give. God sees the heart with more concern than the gift.

God cannot be bribed. Giving plunder to atone for wrongdoing is a vain and ugly sight. Giving a little ill-gotten money does not redeem the swindler. Defiled hands are not cleansed by handing out money. They were not for Judas.

Giving to the church does not make up for the wrong done to another. It is more important that we first go and be reconciled to the one who has aught against us, and then go and give our offering.

Be somebody! Don't just give something!

To do justice and judgment is more acceptable to the Lord than sacrifice. — 21:3

THE sacrifice of the wicked is an abomination to the Lord. — 15:8

Control Yourself

"I conquered an empire, but I was not able to conquer myself," declared Peter the Great. And he wasn't. In an outburst of fury he slew his own son. When self-control fails, then we have a monster on the loose.

The ancient philosopher Plato said, "For a man to conquer himself is the first and noblest of all virtues."

Life can hold no greater challenge to any person than the contest to control himself.

We need to control ourselves:
— Control our temper.
— Control our speech.
— Control our appetites.
— Control our emotions.

HE that hath no rule over his own spirit is like a city that is broken down, and without walls. — 25:28

HE that is slow to anger is better than the mighty; and he that ruleth his spirit than he that taketh a city. — 16:32

A fool uttereth all his mind: but a wise man keepeth it in till afterward. — 29:11

HE that is slow to wrath is of great understanding: but he that is hasty of spirit exalteth folly. — 14:29

Refuse to Wrong Yourself

Things go wrong for the person who does wrong. This is the way he wrongs himself. He brings on troubles by violating the rules of God. If we could only understand that the laws of God were given to bless us, not to boss us, not to hurt us!

Transgression is the trespassing of forbidden territory, and the history of man proves the way is hard. He who travels it does not come out unscathed. We can't walk on coals and not be burned. When we crucify ourselves on a cross of sin, the nails may be drawn, but the scars remain. We can't sow sin and reap elevation. The sinner is his own destruction and his own reproach.

The best commentary on the ruin wrought by sin is the sinner himself. The Prodigal Son is an unimpeachable example. Bankrupt, broken and debauched, he returned home to his father with this tragic confession: "I am no more worthy to be called thy son: make me as one of thy hired servants."

> But he that sinneth against me wrongeth his own soul: all they that hate me love death. — 8:36
>
> Good understanding giveth favor: but the way of the transgressor is hard. — 13:15

Stay on the Side of God

*My concern is not whether God is on our side;
my great concern is to be on God's side, for God
is always right.*
— Abraham Lincoln

Man is endowed with volition. God has given us the will to obey His will. Let His choice be our choice. Choose to be on His side.

As man reaches up, he needs a hand to meet; without it he slips down, without it he cuts off his own hands.

In measuring man, God puts the tape around the motives — keep your intents set on Him.

God is our provider, our protector, our counselor, our consoler, our rock and our refuge. Draw near to Him and He will draw near to you. Be on His side, at His side. Walk with Him.

Lest I be full, and deny thee, and say, Who is the Lord? or lest I be poor, and steal, and take the name of thy God in vain. — 30:9

A good man obtaineth favor of the Lord. — 12:2

A woman that feareth the Lord, she shall be praised. — 31:30

Appear Smart by Talking Less

Consider the parrot — much talking does not necessarily indicate much thinking.

Never be one of whom it is said, "His speech revealed his ignorance." By withholding our comments, our associates won't know that we don't know. They will count us a person of knowledge, all because we kept silent. And that is smart — smart enough not to show our ignorance, which is a lot smarter than some people.

Let our brain have an understanding before it has a tongue; and when stupidity seeks expression, let us close our lips a little tighter.

EVEN a fool, when he holdeth his peace, is counted wise: and he that shutteth his lips is esteemed a man of understanding. — 17:28

IN the multitude of words there wanteth not sin: but he that refraineth his lips is wise. — 10:19

THE wicked is snared by the transgression of his lips: but the just shall come out of trouble. — 12:13

HE that keepeth his mouth keepeth his life: but he that openeth wide his lips shall have destruction. — 13:3

A man hath joy by the answer of his mouth: and a word spoken in due season, how good is it! — 15:23

Avoid Laughing at Sin

Sin is too serious and personal to laugh at. There is no way to deride sin without jeering at the failure of somebody, yourself or some other person.

He who laughs at sin may later cry in sin. For sin, like a spoiled child, is emboldened with laughter. There is enough fleeting pleasure in sin without laughing at it, and enough lasting sorrow in it without mockingly courting it.

O the curse of mocking sin! That we could call it fun! It is just as untimely as it is for the condemned man to laugh on death row.

Let us profit from Solomon's timely summations:

FOOLS make a mock at sin: but among the righteous there is favor. — 14:9

RIGHTEOUSNESS exalteth a nation: but sin is a reproach to any people. — 14:34

THE thought of foolishness is sin: and the scorner is an abomination to men. — 24:9

Refuse to Slander Any Person

Freedom does not mean the right to turn the tongue loose in venomous lies. No one has the right to open a ready mouth and unloose a calumnious tongue.

Any person whose heart has been pierced by the bloody tongue of slander understands the pain more fully than the person who has never been bled by it.

It is the blackest viciousness for a person to engage in a pastime which helps not him and hurts another. It could bring delight to only a fallen nature.

> *Who steals my purse steals trash;*
> *'tis something, nothing;*
> *'Twas mine, 'tis his, and has*
> *been slave to thousands;*
> *But he that filches my good name*
> *Robs me of that which not enriches him,*
> *And makes me poor indeed.*
> — William Shakespeare

Oh, slander, would that those who give you circulation could see their folly and stop you dead in your harm. Calumny lives and grows upon repeating, but dies for lack of tongue. Don't give it yours!

HE that hideth hatred with lying lips, and he that uttereth a slander, is a fool. — 10:18

Don't Kill Yourself With Slothfulness

"Don't kill yourself working," is common advice. But do you ever hear, "Don't kill yourself idling?" Work which brings plenty and happiness is demanding, but idleness which brings want and misery is pernicious. In wasting himself, the sluggard wastes everything about him.

Nothing is as defeating as a sleepy attitude toward life. "Being on the ball" makes a whole new ball game, but sleeping in the dugout forfeits the contest.

> THE desire of the slothful killeth him; for his hands refuse to labor. — 21:25

> HE also that is slothful in his work is brother to him that is a great waster. — 18:9

> SLOTHFULNESS casteth into a deep sleep; and an idle soul shall suffer hunger. — 19:15

> I went by the field of the slothful, and by the vineyard of the man void of understanding; and, lo, it was all grown over with thorns, and nettles had covered the face thereof, and the stone wall thereof was broken down. Then I saw, and considered it well: I looked upon it and received instruction. Yet a little sleep, a little slumber, a little folding of the hands to sleep: So shall thy poverty come as one that traveleth; and thy want as an armed man. — 24:30-34

Avoid Strife

We lose the peace of years when we engage in the strife of moments. Strife grows. Leave it off before it gets started. Don't meddle with it. When strife is met with strife, it is like piling wood on a fire — it gets bigger and hotter.

People usually respond like we treat them. Thus,
— Where there is condemnation, be calm.
— Where there is anger, be kind.
— Where there is hate, be loving.
— Where there is injury, be forgiving.

Let us see that if we bite and devour one another we shall be consumed one of another.

THE beginning of strife is as when one letteth out water: therefore leave off contention, before it be meddled with. — 17:14

IT is an honor for a man to cease from strife: but every fool will be meddling. — 20:3

HE that is of a proud heart stirreth up strife. — 28:25

SURELY the churning of milk bringeth forth butter, and the wringing of the nose bringeth forth blood: so the forcing of wrath bringeth forth strife; — 30:33

AS coals are to burning coals, and wood to fire; so is a contentious man to kindle strife. — 26:21

85

Be Slow to Sign Another's Note

Surety often makes one person comfortable in debt and another person uncomfortable in obligation. If we are a surety on a note, we can hardly be sure for ourselves. Certainly, the creditor thinks there is a strong possibility we will have to pay or he would not demand a cosignatory.

So, never sign another's note if we can find anything else to put our name on.

Life is too short to rush it; and nothing makes time pass as fast as binding ourselves on another's note. The ninety days pass so quickly. And if the borrower doesn't clear the obligation, we'll learn that excuses and regrets pay no debts. Then it is ours to pay for nothing we received. And that is hard!

> HE that is surety for a stranger shall smart for it: and he that hateth suretyship is sure. — 11:15
>
> A man void of understanding striketh hands, and becometh surety in the presence of his friends. — 17:18
>
> TAKE his garment that is surety for a stranger. 27:13
>
> BE not thou one of them that strike hands, or of them that are sureties for debts. If thou hast nothing to pay, why should he take away thy bed from under thee? — 22:26,27

Avoid Being Taken

Isn't it funny that nobody wants to be cheated, but that nearly everybody wants to get close to it. There must be something sweet about it in the anticipation, but how bitter is the reality. Therefore:

— When we are being flattered, postpone our decision for a more unimpressive setting. He who is more gullible to flattery is more easily swindled.

— Investigate. Don't buy a pig in a poke. Any person, product, or organization, that cannot stand investigation should be shunned.

— Remember, outward appearances are often deceiving. A pill is sugar-coated.

— Don't be rushed into a decision. Sleep on a proposition. We may see it in a different light in the morning.

— Don't expect something for nothing. Many are defrauded because they want too much for too little, and end up getting too little for too much.

— If we bite with doubts, nibble just a little at first to be sure we are not playing with a baited hook.

EAT thou not the bread of him that hath an evil eye, neither desire thou his dainty meats: For as he thinketh in his heart, so is he: Eat and drink, saith he to thee; but his heart is not with thee. — 23:6,7

Live Today

Three Days talked to a gentleman about living,
    What's best and what's not.
Yesterday said, "I was enough; don't be looking
    For this, that or what."
Tomorrow said, "Wait for me; now is disappointing;
    I'll give you a lot."
Today said, "Past, gone; tomorrow may not be rising.
    Me? I'm all you've got."

                            — L.B.

Today is the day of joy for the happy.

Today is the day of all days for the wise.

Today is the only eternity the prudent has to act.

A world of people occupy the cemeteries. And legions are outside those cities of the dead, but not all people outside are *living* — some are just breathing, waiting for a more opportune time to *live*. A most tragic tragedy! We get to the grave too soon to miss one joy on the way. Live now. Today. Don't settle for the past — it is gone. Don't wait for tomorrow — it is always a day ahead. Common sense dictates that we live today. However, the common practice is: live tomorrow, and live yesterday, but never live today. But reality tells us that today is the only day to live.

BOAST not thyself of tomorrow; for thou knowest not what a day may bring forth. — 27:1

Trust in the Lord

One of the mistakes of men is their failure to put their trust in God. They trust in themselves and fail. They trust in people and are betrayed. They trust in a cause and it folds. Then there is nothing left to sustain them — and they sink.

May the words on our coins become the words in our heart: *In God We Trust.* The way is too hard to try to make it alone or with only humans — we need to lean on Divinity.

Therefore, trust God:
— When our way is dark.
— When our burdens are heavy.
— When our heart bleeds.
— When our job is threatened.
— When our friends are unkind.
— When our enemies persecute.

TRUST in the Lord with all thine heart; and lean not unto thine own understanding. — 3:5

FOR the Lord shall be thy confidence, and shall keep thy foot from being taken. — 3:26

EVERY word of God is pure: he is a shield unto them that put their trust in him. — 30:5

Be Trustworthy

Trust cannot be produced where there is no basis to support it. Franklin D. Roosevelt said, "Confidence . . . thrives only on honesty, on honor, on the sacredness of obligations, on faithful protection and on unselfish performance. Without them it cannot live."

It is assuring to be associated with a person so trustworthy that we feel safe with him around, assured that he will neither cheat us nor betray us, confident that he won't let us down. We can trust him, whether it be to look after our money or our reputation. We don't have to cut the cards when he deals. That's the person to be — what we prefer in another.

> CONFIDENCE in an unfaithful man in time of trouble is like a broken tooth, and a foot out of joint. — 25:19
>
> HE that walketh uprightly walketh surely: but he that perverteth his ways shall be known. — 10:9
>
> THE integrity of the upright shall guide them: but the perverseness of transgressors shall destroy them. — 11:3
>
> THAT thou mayest walk in the way of good men, and keep the paths of the righteous. — 2:20

Buy the Truth

*The high minded man must care more for truth
than for what people think.*
— Aristotle

To know the truth is easier than buying it; ah, what
we have to give up to buy it: partisanship, blind
loyalties, popularity, friends and relatives.

In buying truth, sometimes it is necessary to part
company with the masses and walk a lonely road; for
truth does not always keep company with the majori-
ty. We don't make truth by popular vote. It is not
altered by the ignorance or fickleness of man. Truth
is no respecter of persons; it is what it is regardless of
its advocates or opponents. And when we go in search
of it, examine it — not the people. We don't always
find it where we expect it.

Error often goes on parade with all the glamour and
glory of a military band amidst the flags, salutes and
confetti, and then in time limps down some back alley
like a consumptive bunch of freaks. So, in buying
truth, don't be persuaded by the noise and fanfare of
the occasion. And when you buy it, never sell it.

This takes character.

BUY the truth, and sell it not. — 23:23

91

Be Visionary

It is always wise to look ahead, and still wiser to look so far ahead that we see what others don't see. This will enable us to push ahead of those with short foresight.

We will never be bigger than the things we see — nor the things we do. The life of a person is his visions plus his plans for realizing them.

When vision and will are short, death begins. Poor vision and weak will are deadly; under their dominance churches, businesses and communities have died. The world is greatly in debt to men and women who saw what others didn't and who did what others wouldn't.

There are many glorious and lucrative opportunities barely showing in the distance. We need to look far to see them, and work hard to reach them. For they exist only to those who see them and seek them.

WHERE there is no vision, the people perish. — 29:18

SHE considereth a field, and buyeth it: with the fruit of her hands she planteth a vineyard. — 31:16

Avoid Wastefulness

Wastefulness has a high price. Students of economics know it.

The president of a big company said, "We don't start to practice thrift by saving pennies; we start by saving mills."

Many of the poor have thrown enough into the alley to put them on easy street. They found that it took more discipline to keep than to get, that it is harder to save than to earn. Without caring for what one has, none can be rich; and with it, few can be poor.

Frugality for the sake of miserly hoarding is no doubt wrong, but frugality for the sake of independence is wise and right. It is the handmaid of plenty. It supplies the cupboard to which we may later go.

> HE also that is slothful in his work is brother to him that is a great waster. — 18:9

> THE slothful man roasteth not that which he took in hunting: but the substance of a diligent man is precious. — 12:27

> THERE is treasure to be desired and oil in the dwelling of the wise; but a foolish man spendeth it up. — 21:20

Establish Yourself With Wisdom

Wisdom knows what to do. Skill knows how to do it.

Wisdom solves problems that gold or silver cannot handle. It gives a security they are helpless to offer. It promotes honor beyond their power to aid.

Nothing is comparable to the sagacious insight which empowers man to act wisely. It enables him to pick his way through an outrageous maze of disastrous paths. And in the long run, no person can prosper out of proportion to the quality and quantity of wisdom he exercises.

> THROUGH wisdom is a house builded; and by understanding it is established. — 24:3

> HAPPY is the man that findeth wisdom, and the man that getteth understanding: For the merchandise of it is better than the merchandise of silver, and the gain thereof than fine gold. — 3:13,14

> WISDOM is the principal thing; therefore get wisdom: and with all thy getting get understanding. Exalt her, and she shall promote thee: she shall bring thee to honor, when thou dost embrace her. She shall give to thine head an ornament of grace: a crown of glory shall she deliver to thee. — 4:7-9

> HE that handleth a matter wisely shall find good. — 16:20